Dr Kathryn Senior is a former biomedical research scientist who studied at Cambridge University for a degree in pathology and a doctorate in microbiology. After four years in research she joined the world of publishing as an editor of children's science books. She has written **Medicine** in the *Timelines* series and **The X-Ray Picture Book of Your Body**. Dr Senior is now a freelance writer and editor.

Nick Hewetson was educated in Sussex at Brighton Technical School and studied illustration at Eastbourne College of Art. He has since illustrated a wide variety of children's books.

David Salariya was born in Dundee, Scotland. He has illustrated a wide range of books on botanical, historical and mythical subjects. He has designed and created the award winning *Timelines*, *New View*, *X-Ray Picture Book* and *Inside Story* series and many other books for publishers in the UK and abroad. He lives in Brighton with his wife, the illustrator Shirley Willis, and their son Jonathan.

Editor: Karen Barker

© The Salariya Book Company Ltd
MCMXCVIII

Created, designed and produced by

THE SALARIYA BOOK COMPANY LTD
25 Marlborough Place,
Brighton BN1 1UB

ISBN 0 7500 2582 4

Published in 1998 by
MACDONALD YOUNG BOOKS
an imprint of Wayland Publishers Ltd
61 Western Road
Hove BN3 1JD

You can find Macdonald Young Books on the internet at http://www.myb.co.uk

A CIP catalogue record for this book is available from the British Library.

Printed in Belgium.

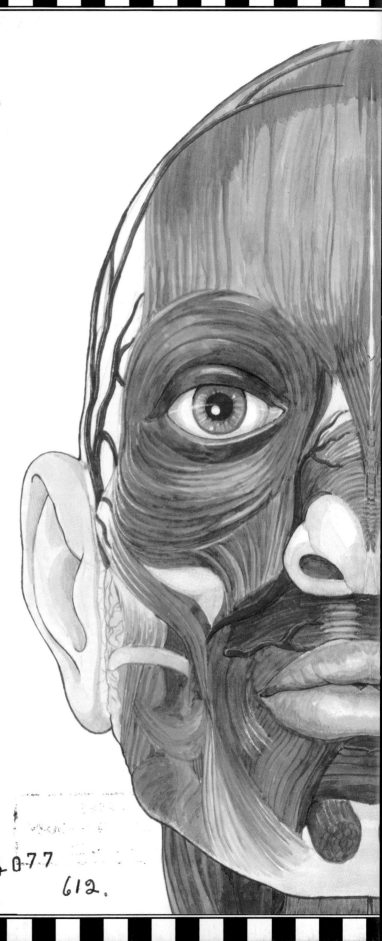

CHECKERS
THE BODY

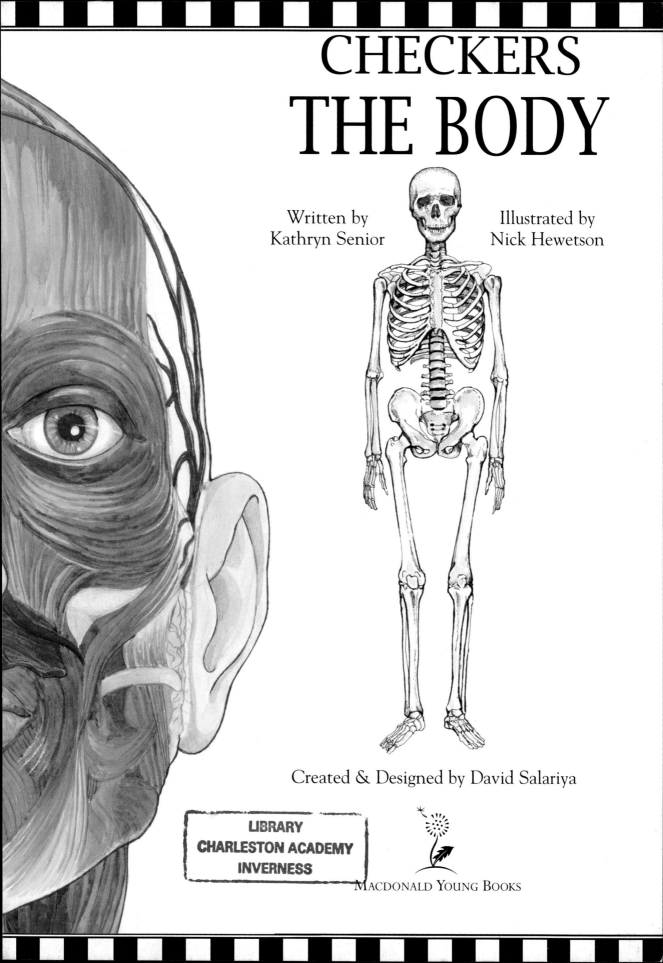

Written by
Kathryn Senior

Illustrated by
Nick Hewetson

Created & Designed by David Salariya

MACDONALD YOUNG BOOKS

Contents

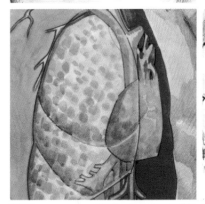

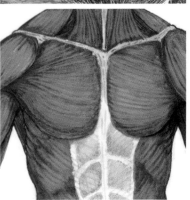

Contents

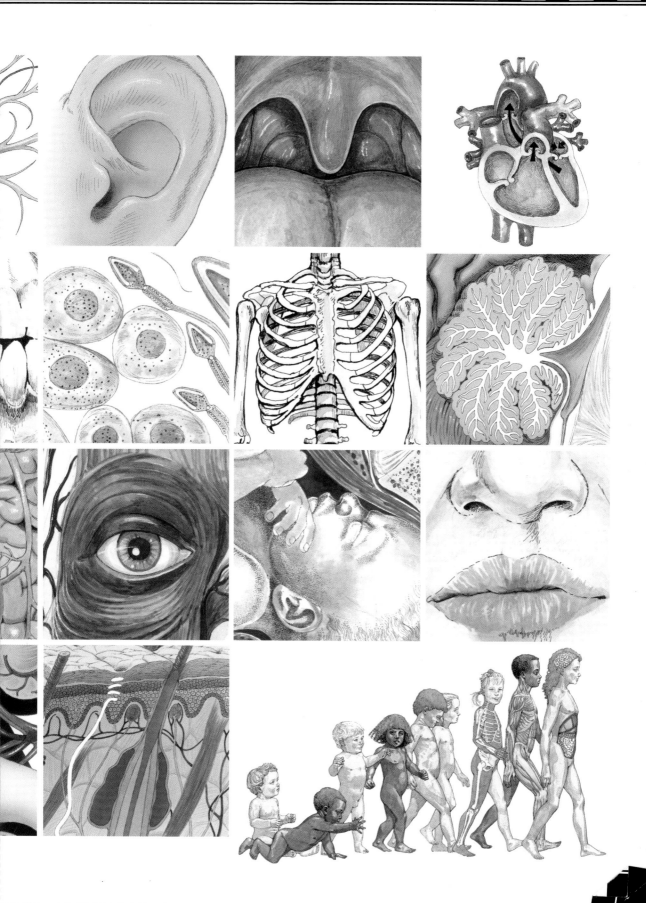

Skin

Skin is the tough wrapping that covers most of the body. It protects the inside of the body against knocks and bumps. Skin stops the body drying out in the sun and prevents water entering the body when in a bath or caught in the rain.

The skin is an organ – the largest organ of the body. It helps to keep the temperature of the body at the right level. When it gets too hot, sweat glands in the skin release salty water onto the surface. This evaporates to cool the body down. If the body gets cold the tiny hairs in the skin stand up and goosepimples appear. These trap a thin layer of air around the body which stops it losing heat.

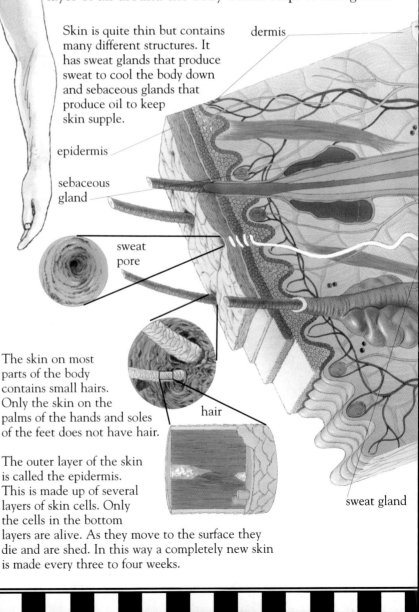

Skin is quite thin but contains many different structures. It has sweat glands that produce sweat to cool the body down and sebaceous glands that produce oil to keep skin supple.

dermis

epidermis

sebaceous gland

sweat pore

hair

sweat gland

The skin on most parts of the body contains small hairs. Only the skin on the palms of the hands and soles of the feet does not have hair.

The outer layer of the skin is called the epidermis. This is made up of several layers of skin cells. Only the cells in the bottom layers are alive. As they move to the surface they die and are shed. In this way a completely new skin is made every three to four weeks.

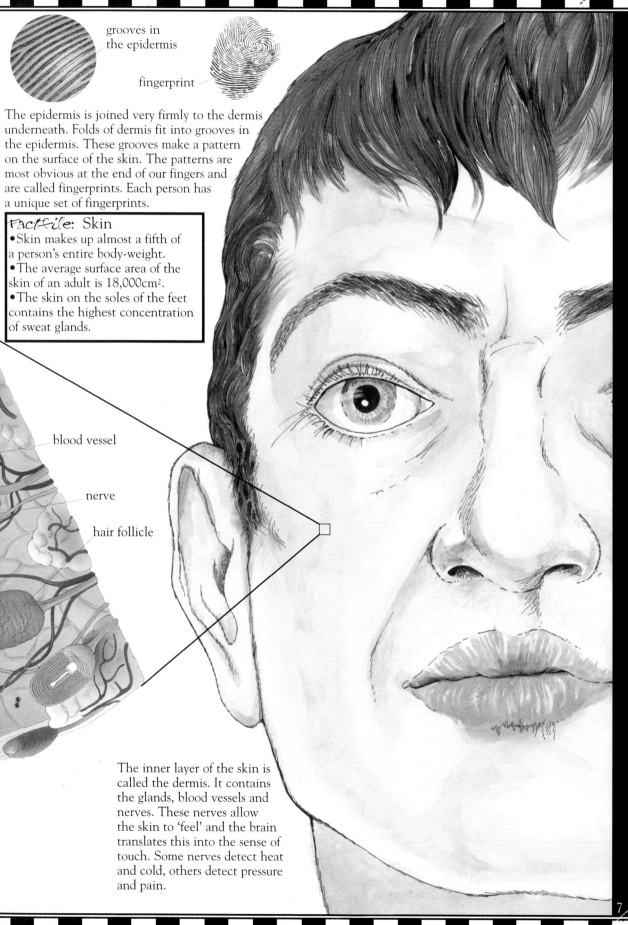

grooves in the epidermis

fingerprint

The epidermis is joined very firmly to the dermis underneath. Folds of dermis fit into grooves in the epidermis. These grooves make a pattern on the surface of the skin. The patterns are most obvious at the end of our fingers and are called fingerprints. Each person has a unique set of fingerprints.

Factfile: Skin
• Skin makes up almost a fifth of a person's entire body-weight.
• The average surface area of the skin of an adult is 18,000cm^2.
• The skin on the soles of the feet contains the highest concentration of sweat glands.

blood vessel

nerve

hair follicle

The inner layer of the skin is called the dermis. It contains the glands, blood vessels and nerves. These nerves allow the skin to 'feel' and the brain translates this into the sense of touch. Some nerves detect heat and cold, others detect pressure and pain.

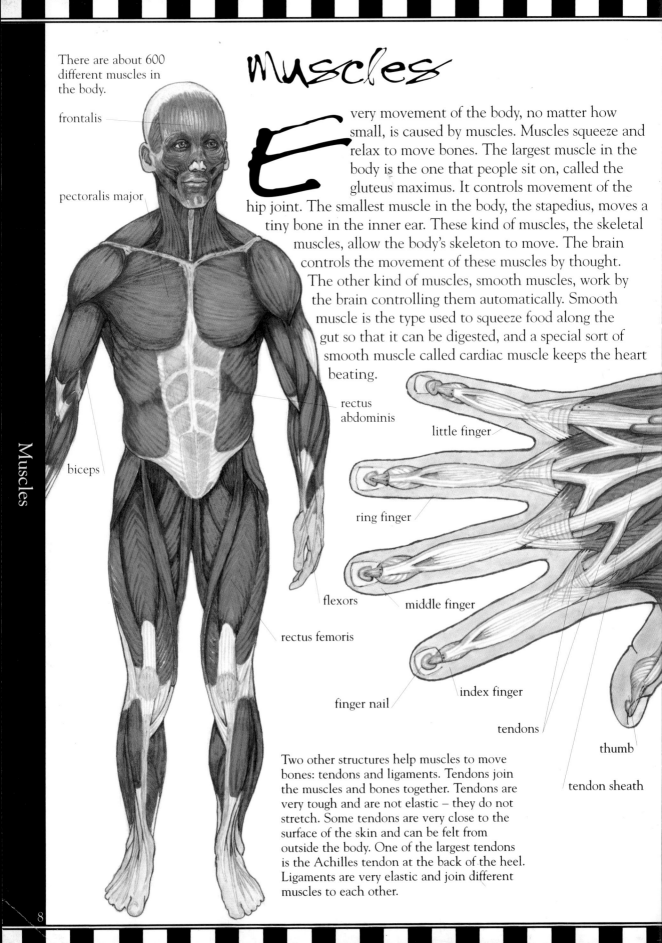

Muscles

There are about 600 different muscles in the body.

frontalis

pectoralis major

Every movement of the body, no matter how small, is caused by muscles. Muscles squeeze and relax to move bones. The largest muscle in the body is the one that people sit on, called the gluteus maximus. It controls movement of the hip joint. The smallest muscle in the body, the stapedius, moves a tiny bone in the inner ear. These kind of muscles, the skeletal muscles, allow the body's skeleton to move. The brain controls the movement of these muscles by thought. The other kind of muscles, smooth muscles, work by the brain controlling them automatically. Smooth muscle is the type used to squeeze food along the gut so that it can be digested, and a special sort of smooth muscle called cardiac muscle keeps the heart beating.

rectus abdominis

little finger

ring finger

biceps

middle finger

flexors

rectus femoris

index finger

finger nail

tendons

thumb

Two other structures help muscles to move bones: tendons and ligaments. Tendons join the muscles and bones together. Tendons are very tough and are not elastic – they do not stretch. Some tendons are very close to the surface of the skin and can be felt from outside the body. One of the largest tendons is the Achilles tendon at the back of the heel. Ligaments are very elastic and join different muscles to each other.

tendon sheath

The face is made up of many different muscles. These work together to make the fine movements that allow so many facial expressions. It takes the action of 43 separate muscles to look cross, but a beaming smile uses only 17 muscles.

Tendons take up less space than muscles and are often found in parts of the body that contain a lot of joints. The hand, for example, which has 15 joints, contains many tendons. These are connected to the bones in the fingers but they are powered by muscles further up the arm.

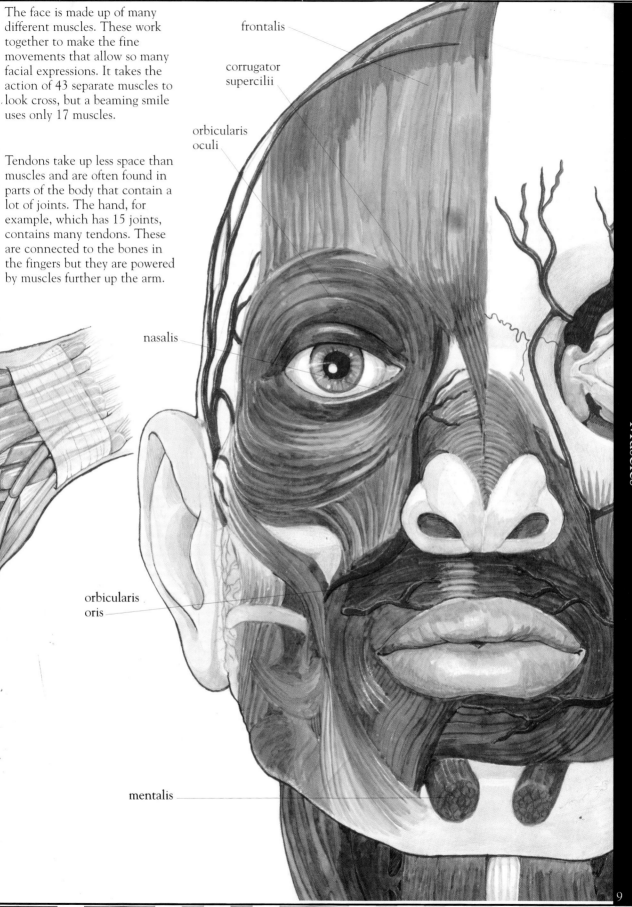

frontalis

corrugator supercilii

orbicularis oculi

nasalis

orbicularis oris

mentalis

Bones

skull

collar bone

rib

sternum

humerus

vertebrae

pelvis

ulna

radius

femur

patella

tibia

fibula

ankle joint

The bones in the body make up the skeleton. Bones often have both common and scientific names. The bone in the top of the leg, for example, is commonly called the thigh bone but it is also known as the femur. The names of some of the other bones are shown on the skeleton on the left. The skeleton is a bit like scaffolding inside the body, supporting all of its parts.

Different parts of the body have different types of bones. The bones in the skull are flat plates. They protect the head against knocks. The long bones in the arms and legs are hollow and contain bone marrow. They support the body but they also have another job to do. The bone marrow makes cells which form an important part of your blood.

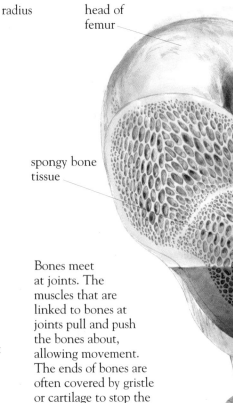

head of femur

spongy bone tissue

Bones meet at joints. The muscles that are linked to bones at joints pull and push the bones about, allowing movement. The ends of bones are often covered by gristle or cartilage to stop the ends rubbing together.

- The skeleton of an average adult has 206 bones.
- At birth, a baby has about 350 separate bones but some of these fuse together as it grows.
- The skull is made up of 29 bones.
- The face contains 14 bones.
- The skeleton does not stop growing until the age of 20.
- Nearly half the bones in the body are in hands and feet.

The bones of the skull do not move but they show amazing patterns of growth during a lifetime. At birth, the different plates are not joined together. They are separated by gaps called fontanelles. These allow the skull to be squashed during birth without causing damage. As the body grows, the fontanelles close up and the skull bones become fused. During old age the brain shrinks and so does the skull, as bone from the inside of the skull is absorbed by the body.

frontal bone

nasal bone

eye socket

upper jaw

Bones look solid but in actual fact only the outside of them is solid. The inner part of bone looks like a honeycomb (see left), which appears delicate but is actually very strong. The honeycomb effect also makes the bone lighter so that it is easy to move around.

teeth

lower jaw

The neck is where the spine joins the bottom of the brain. The bones which protect the spine are called vertebrae. There are 26 vertebrae down the length of the back with the bottom ones positioned right down in the pelvis.

vertebra

Heart and circulation

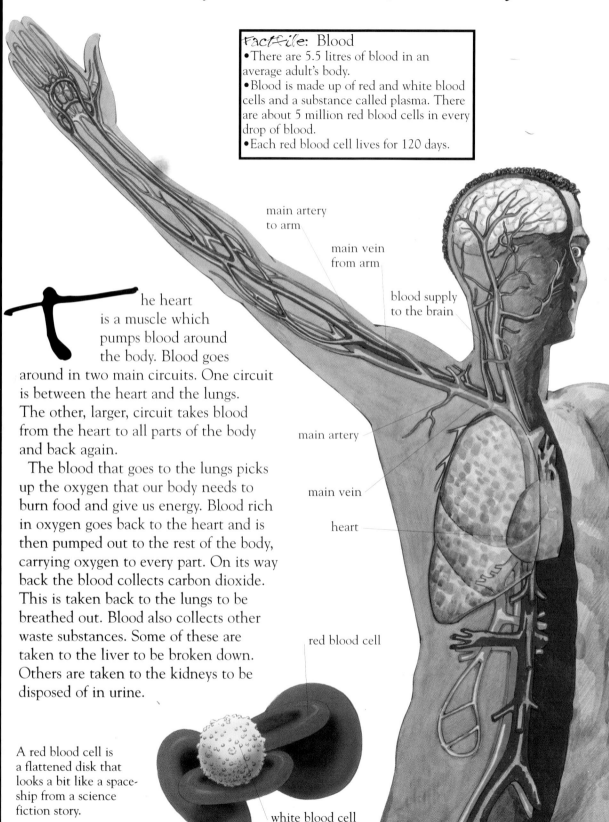

Factfile: Blood
• There are 5.5 litres of blood in an average adult's body.
• Blood is made up of red and white blood cells and a substance called plasma. There are about 5 million red blood cells in every drop of blood.
• Each red blood cell lives for 120 days.

main artery to arm

main vein from arm

blood supply to the brain

main artery

main vein

heart

red blood cell

white blood cell

The heart is a muscle which pumps blood around the body. Blood goes around in two main circuits. One circuit is between the heart and the lungs. The other, larger, circuit takes blood from the heart to all parts of the body and back again.

The blood that goes to the lungs picks up the oxygen that our body needs to burn food and give us energy. Blood rich in oxygen goes back to the heart and is then pumped out to the rest of the body, carrying oxygen to every part. On its way back the blood collects carbon dioxide. This is taken back to the lungs to be breathed out. Blood also collects other waste substances. Some of these are taken to the liver to be broken down. Others are taken to the kidneys to be disposed of in urine.

A red blood cell is a flattened disk that looks a bit like a space-ship from a science fiction story.

12

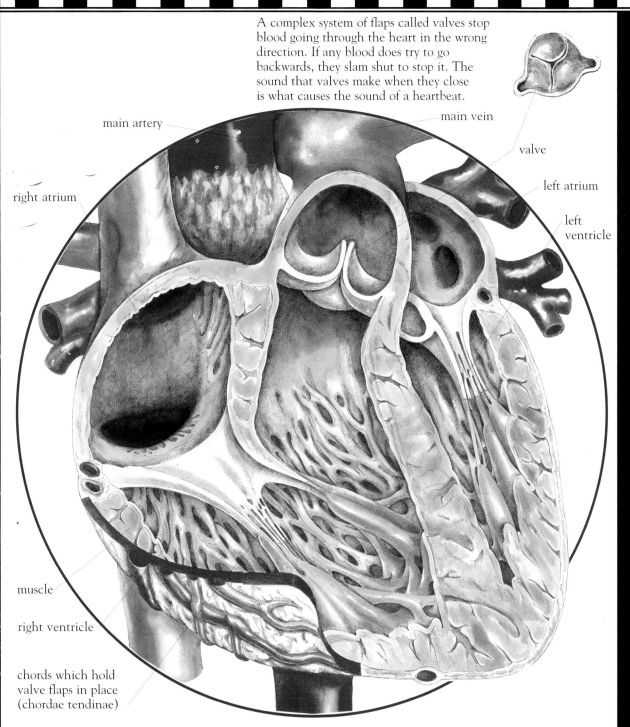

A complex system of flaps called valves stop blood going through the heart in the wrong direction. If any blood does try to go backwards, they slam shut to stop it. The sound that valves make when they close is what causes the sound of a heartbeat.

main artery

main vein

valve

right atrium

left atrium

left ventricle

muscle

right ventricle

chords which hold valve flaps in place (chordae tendinae)

Factfile: Heart and circulation
• The heart of an adult weighs 250-300g and is about the size of a clenched fist.
• When the body is not doing very much, the heart beats about 70 times and pumps a total of 5 litres of blood in every minute.
• If the body exercises by running, the heart beats much faster – up to 150 times per minute – to get more blood and oxygen to the muscles.
• During exercise the heart can pump as much as 20 litres of blood per minute.

The human heart is a double pump. The right ventricle pumps blood to the lungs and the left ventricle pumps blood around the body.
The heart is made of muscle. The muscle is thickest in the left ventricle because this part of the heart has to push blood the greatest distance. The large tubes that bring blood to the heart are called veins and those that take it away again are called arteries.

Lungs and breathing

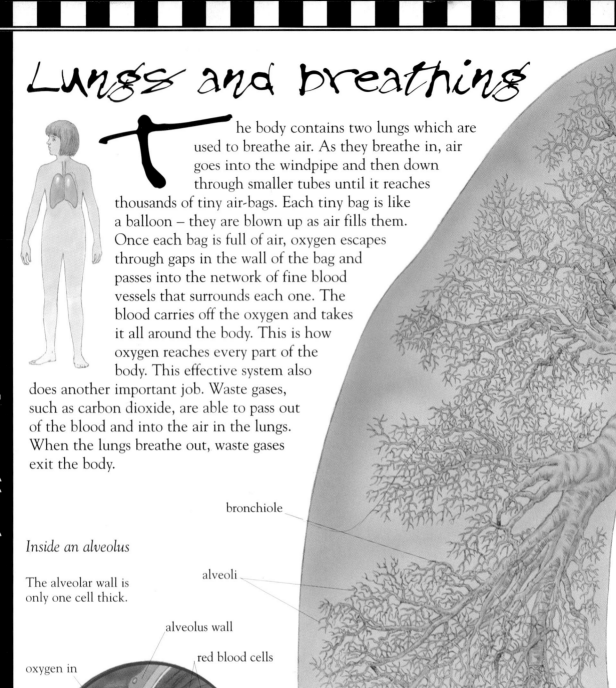

The body contains two lungs which are used to breathe air. As they breathe in, air goes into the windpipe and then down through smaller tubes until it reaches thousands of tiny air-bags. Each tiny bag is like a balloon – they are blown up as air fills them. Once each bag is full of air, oxygen escapes through gaps in the wall of the bag and passes into the network of fine blood vessels that surrounds each one. The blood carries off the oxygen and takes it all around the body. This is how oxygen reaches every part of the body. This effective system also does another important job. Waste gases, such as carbon dioxide, are able to pass out of the blood and into the air in the lungs. When the lungs breathe out, waste gases exit the body.

bronchiole

Inside an alveolus

The alveolar wall is only one cell thick.

alveoli

alveolus wall

red blood cells

oxygen in

carbon dioxide out

blood vessel

wall of blood vessel

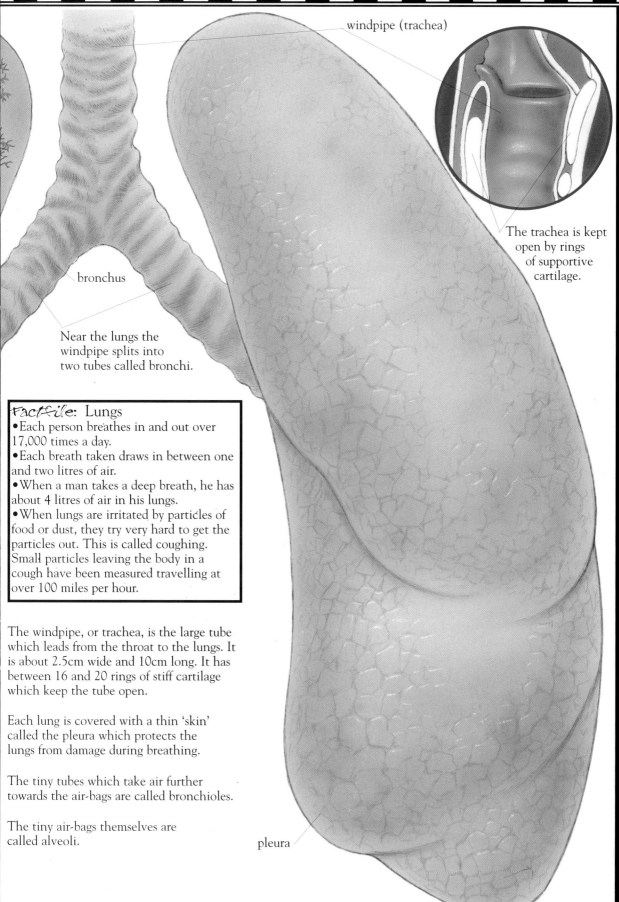

windpipe (trachea)

The trachea is kept
open by rings
of supportive
cartilage.

bronchus

Near the lungs the
windpipe splits into
two tubes called bronchi.

Factfile: Lungs
•Each person breathes in and out over
17,000 times a day.
•Each breath taken draws in between one
and two litres of air.
•When a man takes a deep breath, he has
about 4 litres of air in his lungs.
•When lungs are irritated by particles of
food or dust, they try very hard to get the
particles out. This is called coughing.
Small particles leaving the body in a
cough have been measured travelling at
over 100 miles per hour.

The windpipe, or trachea, is the large tube
which leads from the throat to the lungs. It
is about 2.5cm wide and 10cm long. It has
between 16 and 20 rings of stiff cartilage
which keep the tube open.

Each lung is covered with a thin 'skin'
called the pleura which protects the
lungs from damage during breathing.

The tiny tubes which take air further
towards the air-bags are called bronchioles.

The tiny air-bags themselves are
called alveoli.

pleura

Eating and digestion

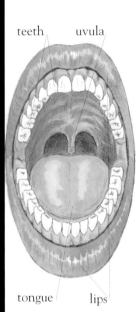

teeth   uvula

tongue   lips

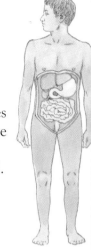

People need to eat food because the body uses it as fuel. The body burns food to get the energy to keep warm, to move and to think. Without food the body would eventually die. When eating, food is first chewed to break it into smaller pieces. When swallowed, the food goes down a tube, called the oesophagus, into the stomach. This bag-like organ mixes up the food with digestive juices. When the food has become complete mush, the stomach squirts it into the first part of the small intestine. This is where most of the food is digested.

Useful substances from the food are taken from the intestine into the blood and carried to all parts of the body. Any unwanted substances continue on into the large intestine. When waste food reaches the end of the large intestine, it leaves the body as faeces.

> **Factfile:** Digestion
> • Saliva in the mouth makes food moist so it can be swallowed. In a lifetime of 70 years, about 20,000 litres of saliva is produced.
> • Almost all of the five to ten litres of water that enters the small intestine every day is taken into the rest of the body.

When empty, the stomach is the same size as a large sausage, but it can stretch to the size of a melon.

Surface of stomach

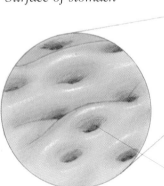

gastric pit

ruga

The digestive system is about nine metres long from one end to the other. Six metres of this is the small intestine which is coiled and twisted to fit into the abdomen.

The liver produces bile which is stored in the gall bladder before going into the small intestine. Bile helps to digest fats.

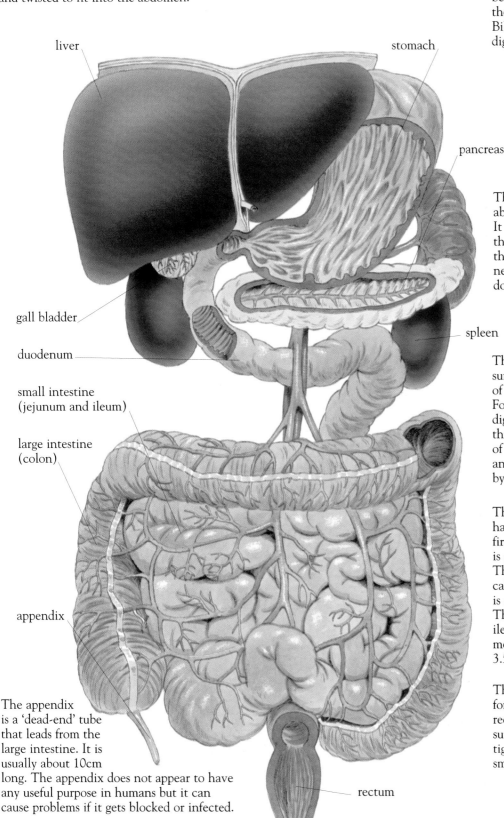

liver

stomach

pancreas

The pancreas is about 15cm long. It produces some of the digestive juices that the intestine needs to break down food.

gall bladder

duodenum

spleen

The intestines are surrounded by lots of blood vessels. Food that has been digested passes through the walls of the intestine and is picked up by the blood.

small intestine (jejunum and ileum)

large intestine (colon)

The small intestine has three parts. The first, the duodenum, is about 25cm long. The middle part, called the jejunum, is about 2.5m long. The last part, the ileum, is the longest, measuring about 3.5m long.

appendix

The large intestine forms a sort of rectangle which surrounds the tightly coiled small intestine.

The appendix is a 'dead-end' tube that leads from the large intestine. It is usually about 10cm long. The appendix does not appear to have any useful purpose in humans but it can cause problems if it gets blocked or infected.

rectum

Kidney

Most people have two kidneys, but it is possible to live a healthy life with only one. The kidneys filter the blood. They allow waste to pass through without losing useful substances such as sugars and water. The waste products that pass through travel down a tube called the ureter and into a storage bag called the bladder This waste fluid is called urine and is let out of the body when people go to the toilet. About 1,200 litres of blood pass through the kidneys every day but the amount of urine produced is much less. Most of the water is taken back into the body by the kidneys so only 1-1.5 litres of urine is produced each day.

A large blood vessel called an artery takes blood into the kidney to be 'cleaned'.

Another sort of blood vessel called a vein takes 'cleaned' blood away from the kidney.

The main part of the kidney contains many complicated filters and tubes. These remove waste products from the blood that passes through. The waste (urine) travels down the ureter to the bladder.

The outside of each kidney is protected by a tough capsule.

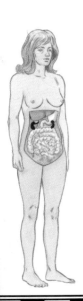

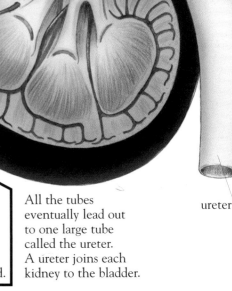

vein

artery

capsule

Factfile: Kidney
• Each kidney is 15cm long and weighs 150g.
• The kidneys control the amount of water and salt in the body.
• The bladder of an adult can hold about 0.25 litres of urine before feeling uncomfortable, and can hold about 0.50 litres before it really has to be emptied.

All the tubes eventually lead out to one large tube called the ureter. A ureter joins each kidney to the bladder.

ureter

Liver

The body has only one liver but it is a large organ. It sits in the middle of the body below the lungs and above the stomach and intestines. The liver does many different things but it has two main jobs. One is to produce chemicals that the body needs, such as hormones and other proteins. The other is to deal with poisons and wastes within the body. It is the liver, for example, that breaks down medicines such as antibiotics and paracetamol. These are very useful, but if they were not broken down after a few hours, they would do the body more harm than good.

The liver also produces a thick green fluid called bile. This is stored in a small bag-like organ just under the liver, called the gall bladder. Bile is very important for digestion because it breaks up the fats that are eaten. This makes it easier for them to be digested in the stomach and intestine.

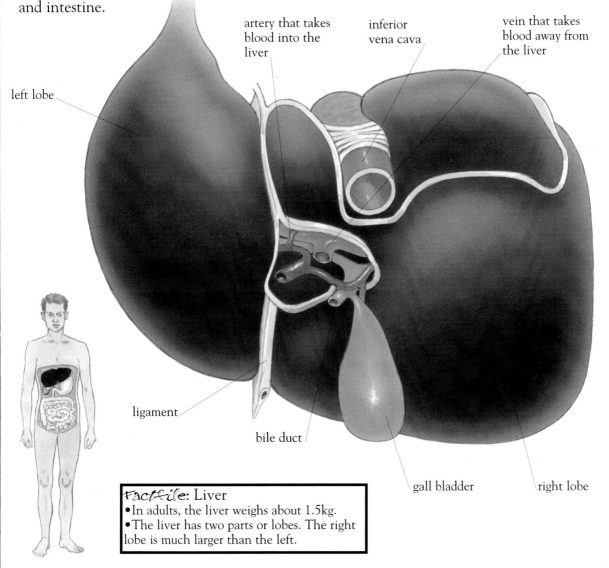

artery that takes blood into the liver

inferior vena cava

vein that takes blood away from the liver

left lobe

ligament

bile duct

gall bladder

right lobe

Factfile: Liver
- In adults, the liver weighs about 1.5kg.
- The liver has two parts or lobes. The right lobe is much larger than the left.

Brain and nervous system

The brain is like a central computer. It controls all parts of the body. It sends and receives messages through long, thin, wire-like structures called nerves. The nerves near the surface of the body spread out like the branches of a tree. The nerves which lead to the brain come together to form a thick trunk of nerves called the spinal cord. This is the main communication channel between the body and the brain. The brain itself is a very complex organ which is grey and wrinkled in appearance. The wrinkled part is call the cerebral cortex. The cortex is the part of the brain that 'thinks' and different parts of it sort out the various types of information that enter it. A part of the cortex at the back of the head, for example, allows us to work out what we are seeing with our eyes.

cerebrum

cerebellum

spinal cord

radial nerve

sciatic nerve

The spinal cord is a column of nerves. It is about 40cm long and runs inside the backbone from the brain to the base of the back.

Nerve cell (neuron)

Nerve cells (right) are the longest cells in the body. Some of the nerve cells which connect toes with the spinal cord are about 1m long.

cell body

dendrite

FactFile: Brain
• After the age of 20, the brain loses 1g in weight every year.
• Eating a peanut gives the brain enough energy to think very hard for two hours.
• An adult's brain is three times heavier than a newborn baby's.

The average weight of an adult human brain is 1.4kg. Men tend to have heavier brains than women. This is because, usually, men are larger than women – it does not mean that there is any difference in intelligence. Some of the most intelligent people in history had smaller than average brains.

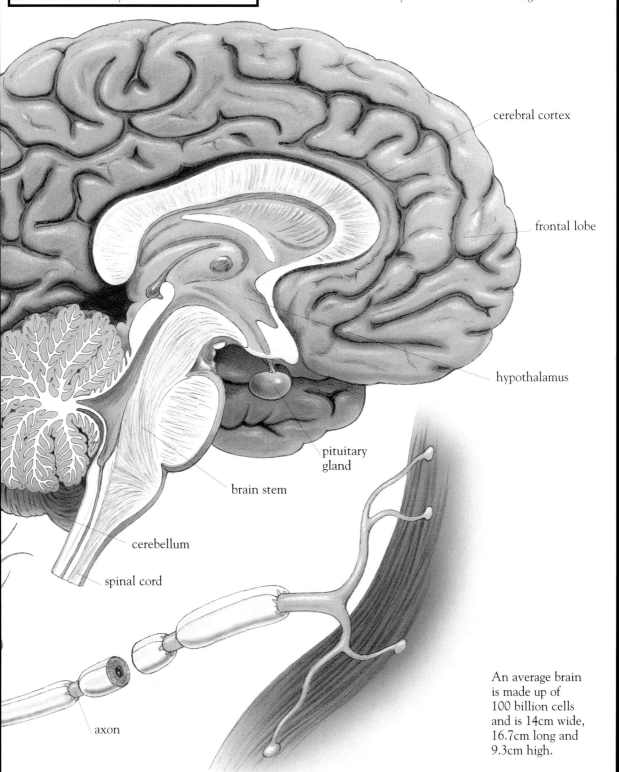

cerebral cortex

frontal lobe

hypothalamus

pituitary gland

brain stem

cerebellum

spinal cord

axon

An average brain is made up of 100 billion cells and is 14cm wide, 16.7cm long and 9.3cm high.

Seeing and hearing

The human head contains two eyes. Each one is shaped like a globe and sits in a hole at the front of the skull, called an orbit. The bone around the hole surrounds most of the eyeball and protects its delicate parts.

Most of the ball of the eye is hidden from view. The part that is visible is just the front of the eyeball which contains the iris and the pupil. The iris is normally coloured brown, blue or green and the pupil is the inner black part which changes size according to the light conditions. In bright light the pupil is small; in dimmer light its size increases.

Factfile: Eye
• Light enters the eye through the pupil.
• The light is focused by a lens and forms an image on the retina at the back of the eyeball. This image is converted into an electrical signal that travels along the optic nerve to the brain. The brain sorts out the signal and is able to 'see' what the eye is looking at.

The outside of the eye is kept moist at all times by tears. The eyelids and eyelashes stop grit and dust entering the eye. Every person has a strong blink reflex – automatic shutting of the eyelids – that stops larger particles damaging the eyes.

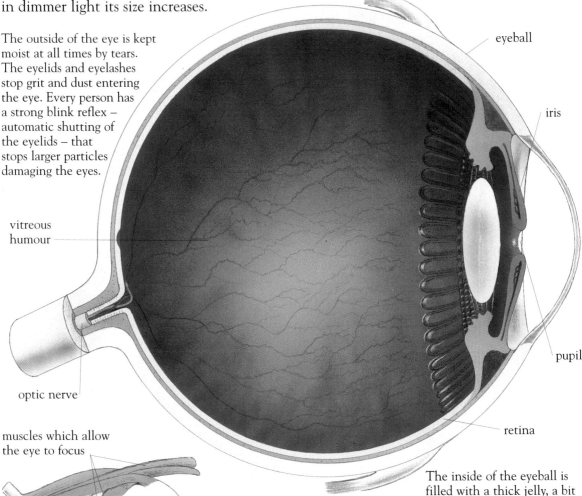

muscle

eyeball

iris

vitreous humour

pupil

optic nerve

retina

muscles which allow the eye to focus

The eyeball is held in place by bands of muscle which can move it in all directions. These enable great movement of the eyes so that a lot can be seen without moving the head.

The inside of the eyeball is filled with a thick jelly, a bit like the white of a raw egg, called the vitreous humour. It helps to cushion the retina and nerves in the eye so that they are not damaged if the head is bumped or knocked.

The outside of the ear is called the pinna. It is made of skin and cartilage and is shaped to gather sound into the ear for clear hearing. Most other mammals' ears are better at doing this than humans'. The ears of a dog, for example, can prick up and swivel to catch sound coming from different directions. An opening in the pinna leads into a complex system of channels and canals which allow hearing and also control the body's sense of balance. Sound waves travel through the bony canal to the ear drum. From here they go to the middle ear where they hit three tiny bones. These bones act as amplifiers, making the original sound 20 times louder. In the inner ear, the amplified sound sets up vibrations in the fluid inside a long coiled tube called the cochlea. These vibrations cause tiny hairs inside the canal to twitch. The hairs change the sound waves into electrical signals and send them to the brain through a large nerve called the auditory nerve.

Outer ear (pinna)

helix

concha

lobule

It is the fluid inside the cochlea which controls the body's sense of balance. When the body moves, the hairs inside the cochlea are made to twitch by the fluid's movement. These twitches send messages to the brain which may conflict with messages coming from other parts of the body, such as the eyes. This results in a feeling of dizziness and perhaps sickness.

cochlea

auditory nerve

the three bones of the middle ear

ear drum

pinna

Eustachian tube

Teeth, taste and smell

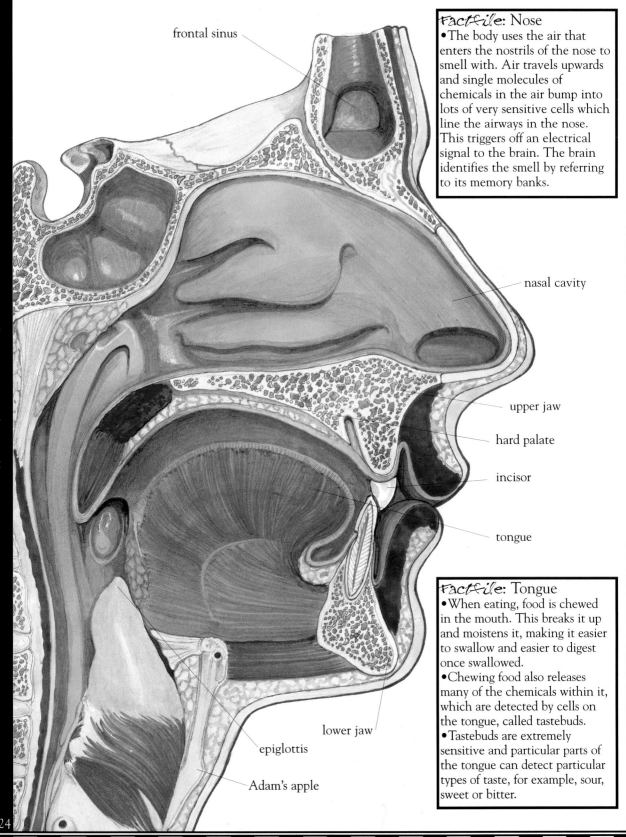

frontal sinus

nasal cavity

upper jaw

hard palate

incisor

tongue

Factfile: Tongue
•When eating, food is chewed in the mouth. This breaks it up and moistens it, making it easier to swallow and easier to digest once swallowed.
•Chewing food also releases many of the chemicals within it, which are detected by cells on the tongue, called tastebuds.
•Tastebuds are extremely sensitive and particular parts of the tongue can detect particular types of taste, for example, sour, sweet or bitter.

lower jaw

epiglottis

Adam's apple

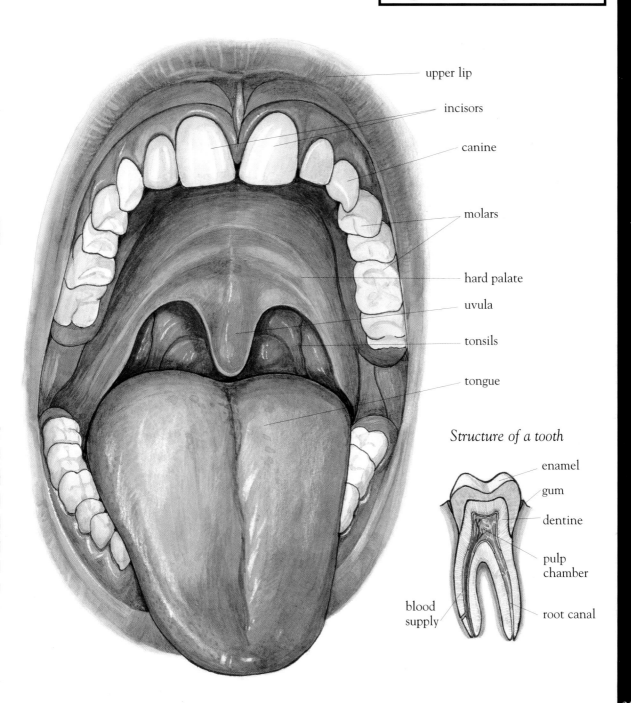

he senses of smell and taste are very closely linked. If a person is blindfolded and also pinches their nose, they will not always be able to tell the difference between a piece of onion placed on their tongue, and a piece of apple. A large part of a human's ability to taste food depends on smelling it at the same time.

Factfile: Teeth
• A human child first starts to grow teeth at about six months old. By the age of two and a half they usually have a full set of first teeth – the milk teeth. These start to fall out at the age of six or seven and, by the age of 12, most people have 28 adult teeth.
• The last four teeth to appear are the 'wisdom' teeth which usually come through between the ages of 18 and 22.

upper lip

incisors

canine

molars

hard palate

uvula

tonsils

tongue

Teeth, taste and smell

Structure of a tooth

enamel

gum

dentine

pulp chamber

blood supply

root canal

Reproduction

labels: sperm, tail of sperm, egg

Every person starts life as a single egg and a single sperm. The egg comes from the mother and the sperm comes from the father. The sperm meets the egg and joins with it (right) inside the mother's body. The fertilised egg that forms then splits into two. These two cells also split into two and this happens repeatedly until the ball of cells begins to resemble a baby.

For the first nine months the baby grows inside the mother's uterus. During these months all the body parts develop until the baby is ready to be born. When the baby is born it is more or less helpless and needs a lot of care and attention. A newborn baby weighs about three kilograms. At first the baby only drinks milk. Most women try to breastfeed their babies, but those who cannot make up special milk in bottles. Either way, the milk contains all the nutrients that the baby needs to grow.

By the age of one, most babies have learnt to crawl or shuffle or even walk. The brain and nerves continue to develop and children gradually become more co-ordinated and able to do things for themselves. Most children reach their final height between the ages of 11 and 18 but the body continues to change and new skills are learned continually throughout life.

The story of a pregnancy

A woman's body undergoes some remarkable changes when she is pregnant. Before the baby starts to grow she looks like this.	During the first three months of pregnancy, the baby grows very fast but there is hardly any sign of this on the outside of the mother.	After about five months, the baby inside the uterus pushes out from between the intestines and the mother now has an obvious 'bump'.	After seven months the woman looks heavily pregnant and the weight of the baby and its pressure on her body will be making her feel tired.	After nine months the woman is very uncomfortable. The baby is so big it squashes her stomach and intestines and rests on the blood vessels and nerves in her back.

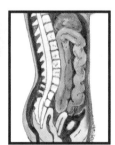 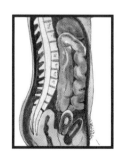 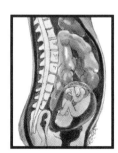 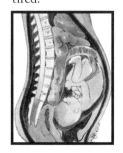 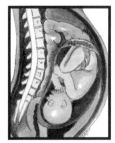

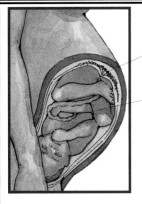

placenta

umbilical cord

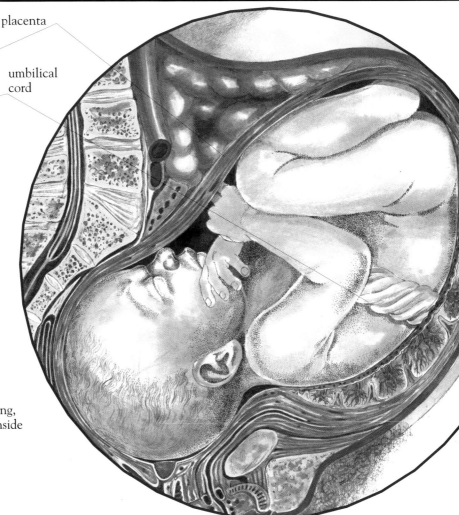

The baby gets food and oxygen from its mother through a spongy structure called the placenta.

The placenta is joined to the baby by the umbilical cord. The belly button marks the place where the cord joined the baby to its mother.

After nine months of growing, the baby is very squashed inside its mother's uterus.

The baby usually faces downwards as it prepares to be born.

Fibre optic cameras have been used to film babies in the uterus sucking their thumb.

Factfile: Reproduction
• On average, a normal pregnancy lasts for 266 days from conception to birth.
• As a baby grows in its mother's uterus, the uterus expands to 1,000 times its non-pregnant volume.
• Every baby starts as a single fertilised egg. Each egg is much smaller than a full-stop and weighs just a fraction of a gram.
• An average new baby measures about 50cm from head to toe and weighs about three and a half kilograms.
• A non-pregnant woman has about five litres of blood in her body, while a woman who is nine months pregnant has six and a half litres of blood.

A newborn baby continues to grow very quickly as it is fed on milk. After about four months, most babies start to eat some solid food as well. During its first year, a baby's weight triples. It also becomes less helpless – most one year-olds can move

themselves around and some can walk. By the age of four, a child can do many of the things an adult can. Children continue to grow and do not reach their final height until they are teenagers. Between the ages of about 10 and 16, a teenager's body matures and prepares to continue the life-cycle, but most people wait until their late twenties or thirties to start their own family.

Running or jogging strengthens the heart and leg muscles and makes the lungs work hard.

Young babies cannot move their body in a co-ordinated way – they must learn to sit up, crawl and walk. As the body matures, such movements become automatic and more complicated exercise like running, dancing or skipping is possible.

Exercise and sleep

A healthy body depends on a variety of good things to eat, plenty of exercise for bones, muscles, heart and lungs, and a good night's sleep.

When running about and playing games, the heart beats more strongly to get more blood pumping around the body. The more active the muscles are, the more fresh blood they need. When exercising regularly, the heart and muscles get stronger and the body gets fitter. Adults who train very hard 'build up' their muscles. This is at its most extreme in weightlifters. Other sportsmen and women, such as marathon runners, may look very thin – their strongest muscle is their heart which does a huge amount of work when they run 26 miles in one race.

Not being able to sleep when you want to is called insomnia. Most people suffer from this from time to time but some people have it every night. Without much needed sleep they toss and turn and when they get up they are tired and irritable.

A newborn baby sleeps for most of the day, but it only
sleeps in short bursts of a few hours at a time. It wakes for milk
every two to three hours at first. By the age of six months most babies
can sleep for eight to 12 hours. Most children continue to need a lot
of sleep until they are about 10 years old. Then they need less, and
most adults can manage with about seven or eight hours sleep
each night. Older people need even less sleep – sometimes
as little as four or five hours.

Body quiz

1. Which is the largest organ in the body?
a) The heart
b) The skin
c) The brain

2. What are the structures that join one muscle to another called?
a) Ligaments
b) Tendons
c) Bones

3. How many bones are there in an average adult skeleton?
a) 206
b) 306
c) 350

4. Which type of blood vessel brings blood to the heart?
a) Arteries
b) White blood cells
c) Veins

5. How fast do particles that leave the body in a cough travel?
a) 10 miles per hour
b) 100 miles per hour
c) 1000 miles per hour

6. What is the longest part of the small intestine called?
a) The duodenum
b) The jejunum
c) The ileum

7. Which one of these jobs is NOT done by the kidneys?
a) Control the amount of water in the body
b) Control the amount of salt in the body
c) Control the digestion of food in the body

8. Which are the longest cells in the body?
a) Nerve cells
b) Bone cells
c) Skin cells

9. How many senses does the body have?
a) 3
b) 5
c) 10

10. What is the structure that joins a baby to its mother before it is born?
a) The placenta
b) The umbilical cord
c) The uterus

Quiz answers are on page 32.

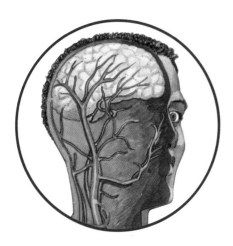

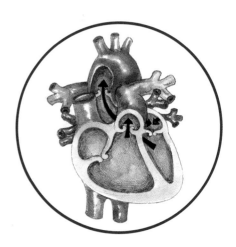

Glossary

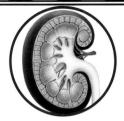 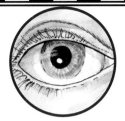 

cardiac The scientific and medical name used to describe the heart. Cardiac muscle is the muscle of the heart and cardiac arrest is when the heart stops beating.

cartilage A spongy material that surrounds the end of bones where they meet other bones at joints. It protects the ends from rubbing together when they move.

cell The smallest unit of life. Everything in the body is either made up of cells or is made of things produced by cells. Cells in different parts of the body are specialised because they do special jobs. Nerve cells, for example, are long and thin and carry electrical messages.

circulation The term used to describe the way blood travels around the body. It does not travel in a circle but through many complicated circuits so that every part of the body constantly receives a supply of fresh blood.

digestion The process that the body uses to break down food. Chemicals are released throughout the digestive system to break down different types of food. The resulting molecules are then taken into the blood and carried around the body. Most digestion happens in the small intestine.

glands Organs that produce chemicals useful to the body, i.e., sweat glands in the skin produce sweat, the pancreas produces hormones and chemicals for digestion, and glands in the corner of the eyes produce tears.

ligaments The elastic rods that join one muscle to another.

nerves Special body structures that pass messages around the body. The brain, the centre of the nervous system, processes all the messages and controls all the functions of the body.

organ A type of structure in the body that carries out a complicated job. Examples of organs are: the heart, the kidneys, the liver and the skin. Structures that hold the body together, such as ligaments and cartilage, are not organs.

pregnancy The nine month period during which a baby grows and develops inside its mother.

skeletal muscle The type of muscle that is joined to the bones of the body and allows movement. This kind of muscle is controlled by thinking about what the body wants to do. For example, to jump up and down, a person consciously moves the muscles in their legs and feet.

smooth muscle The type of muscle that works without the brain consciously thinking about it. Smooth muscles move food along the intestines and keep the heart beating.

tendon Tough, rigid rods that join muscles to bones.

waste Substances that the body does not need. Waste produced by chemical processes in the body is removed from the blood by the 'cleaning' action of the kidneys. It then leaves the body in urine. Food waste (what is left after digestion) passes through the large intestine and then leaves the body as faeces.

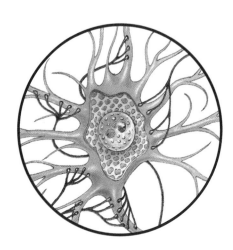

Index

Index